THE REBIRTH OF MY SOUL, 2ND EDITION

AIJA M. BUTLER

1 | *I choose to speak the words of my heart,*
for fear they will be lost in the confines
of my mind, thus clouding my vision

THE REBIRTH OF MY SOUL, 2ND EDITION

AIJA M. BUTLER

*I choose to speak the words of my heart,
for fear they will be lost in the confines
of my mind, thus clouding my vision*

DECLARATION

I share these stories for the sole purpose of inspiring others not everyone gets to walk through fire and live to tell about it.

I choose to speak the words of my heart, for fear they will be lost in the confines of my mind, thus clouding my vision

MY AFFIRMATION

Just as salt burns open wounds. The mind can be corrupted by thoughts, and by persons that look to downplay your desires, dreams, and goals.

We throw salt into our own paths, by letting our fear of the unknown cloud our visions as well as others open our wounds, and salt our dreams. Thus they become dreams deferred.

My inspirational bout is a collection of notes, advice, and keys to success. Without mistakes and failures one cannot become successful.

Tour my journey through sickness and health, which led me to a new beginning, and the rebirth of my soul.

My mistakes and shortcomings are no longer my failures. They have become life experiences.

I choose to speak the words of my heart, for fear they will be lost in the confines of my mind, thus clouding my vision

THE REBIRTH OF MY SOUL, 2ND EDITION

AIJA M. BUTLER

Experiences I will now share with you. As you too, strive for bigger and brighter futures.

Written Works of Aija M. Butler

I choose to speak the words of my heart, for fear they will be lost in the confines of my mind, thus clouding my vision

THE REBIRTH OF MY SOUL, 2ND EDITION

AIJA M. BUTLER

TABLE OF CONTENTS

I choose to speak the words of my heart, for fear they will be lost in the confines of my mind, thus clouding my vision

7 | *I choose to speak the words of my heart, for fear they will be lost in the confines of my mind, thus clouding my vision*

THE REBIRTH OF MY SOUL, 2ND EDITION

Nurture and Development

I made a list

Auxiliary Labels Proceed with Caution

Want To Make a Bet

8 *I choose to speak the words of my heart, for fear they will be lost in the confines of my mind, thus clouding my vision*

THE REBIRTH OF MY SOUL, 2ND EDITION

AIJA M. BUTLER

I choose to speak the words of my heart, for fear they will be lost in the confines of my mind, thus clouding my vision

I Don't Have Time

Fantasy Land

Goldmine

Honorable Discharge

If it can't be Helped

2003 At Deaths Door

Mrs. Doubt-fire

Abandoned Ship

Arts and Creativity

Your Level of Understanding

A Long for the Ride

Swag

Parental Advisory

Scary Movie

*I choose to speak the words of my heart,
for fear they will be lost in the confines
of my mind, thus clouding my vision*

I choose to speak the words of my heart, for fear they will be lost in the confines of my mind, thus clouding my vision

THE REBIRTH OF MY SOUL

I choose to speak the words of my heart, for fear they will be lost in the confines of my mind, thus clouding my vision

INTRODUCTION

UNDER SIEGE

The winter winds blew in and I took refuge under a blanket. My laptop was on its full charge and I was ready to unleash the beast that lay dormant during summer. The wake always enters in the cold. The heat of the sun fry's my brain and summer's end is celebrated.

During my slumber I question my very existence. Troubled with the creativity of the Aquarian mind I often jump from high levels into full on projects which never seem to see the end. Times have now changed, however. My mind has been opened to new ventures.

I am excited, in fact, that I have the patience to see things through. However, nasty and cut throat the world of any venture

I choose to speak the words of my heart, for fear they will be lost in the confines of my mind, thus clouding my vision

may be, I am standing on my own two feet accepting and battling my adversaries.

My heart and mind are at constant war. The sensitivity's I often wear on my sleeve peek when I am trying hard to shield them from preying eyes. I hold my head high and cry during the dark nights. Wishing my foe well, keeping them close in mind and reach. I am able to continue in challenge.

The war is on. The Rebirth is here challenging my most dreadful moments of fear and failure. I am constantly taunted by the fallen angel on the right of me and my savior on my left. Hunching over often buried by the troubled times of this life full of responsibility and burden I sift to find those moments of love and laughter.

I find them close, as my children's bright eyes glisten, I remember. I am again born and ready to fight the good fight. Once again remembering why I am truly here.

I choose to speak the words of my heart, for fear they will be lost in the confines of my mind, thus clouding my vision

AIJA M. BUTLER

Running the race, with a winner's circle
chanting my way to the finish line, to finish
is my goal, not necessarily to win.

*I choose to speak the words of my heart,
for fear they will be lost in the confines
of my mind, thus clouding my vision*

NO AUTOGRAPHS PLEASE

I remember the day I got released from the hospital. I put on my Sunday best. A two piece pajama set and a matching scarf. I was so afraid to leave that I cried every five minutes.

Having the tubes removed from my body's orifices was almost more painful than having them put in. Apart of me thought I would die instantly if they were disturbed.

The hospital staff was lined up from my door to the entrance of the elevators on the fifth floor. I couldn't believe the turn out. My departure was an event. The clapping and well wishes began, as I rolled from my room. I felt overwhelmed with emotion.

I choose to speak the words of my heart, for fear they will be lost in the confines of my mind, thus clouding my vision

I held my breath as I entered the elevator. I started to feel pressure in my chest. The anticipation of the night air was overwhelming. I'd spent what seemed to be a lifetime in confinement. I was afraid to breathe, for fear the air would cut my lungs. My throat was still recovering from the tubes removed from my throat. My nose had large scabs in its canal that hurt to the touch. My lips were dry, and my mouth begged for ice.

This was the beginning of my life. I was so unsure of my existence. Furthermore, fear of my abilities to act and feel as an adult; add insecurities to my reconnecting with my daughter. Now walking and mumbling her first words.

I was famous to those in the medical field. I was nobody to the real world. Reality quickly sunk in. There set the pace for my earning my keep, and taking my place on earth. I was alone and very afraid.

I choose to speak the words of my heart, for fear they will be lost in the confines of my mind, thus clouding my vision

AIJA M. BUTLER

REMEMBER THE CAUSE... CONTINUE THE FIGHT...

I spent years trying to please my friends and family. It's hard to be an individual at times. The worries of acceptance hinder growth. Soon you find yourself in search of approval in every aspect of your life. Will my parents and family accept my career choices, significant other, my faults, failures, success even?

My anxiety level burst into flames and I ran around my space on earth like a chicken with its head cut off. I was confused, fearful of success and failure just the same. What an odd combination? I often ask myself how one could possibly fear success? It is such a stifling disease. I now…, I recognize that the true issue with

I choose to speak the words of my heart, for fear they will be lost in the confines of my mind, thus clouding my vision

success isn't the notion at all. It's the responsibility that comes with it. This is what I feared.

Before my bout with disease I was confident. I can still hear my heels hitting the pavement and my briefcase flying in the wind, as I walk confidently down the city streets of Downtown Los Angeles. I am smiling as I type this. The wind tickled the scalp of my natural mane, my skin glowed, and I was free of these nasty scars that sit right between my eyes.

I chose to write this book above my list of written works because I wanted to produce a memoir that wasn't just a good read but a companion. Our natural companions are often ignored, the conscience. I will be first to admit that I seek counsel with mine on a daily basis. We argue my plan of action, my depressive state of mind when awakened by disease, and during my times of trial my will to live.

I choose to speak the words of my heart, for fear they will be lost in the confines of my mind, thus clouding my vision

AIJA M. BUTLER

The Rebirth of My Soul is this journey I happened upon. I didn't choose the fight, but I chose to fight the battle just the same. I am often weary. My lungs close during the winter season and my temperature causes me to seek immediate medical attention.

Today I am different. I worry of infection, dust, and grime. I work on stress and anxiety, fearing my last breath will slip from my parted lips and my work is not done. These worries and concerns are what this journey is about. I fight to rid myself of these fears, the same fear of success less, the same fear of abandonment, and ill remarks towards the path I've chosen from friends and family. Each of us will taste death, each day is not promised.

I do believe my goal of each day forward, is to smile as I inhale and relax as I exhale, thankful that God has blessed me with a new day.

I wanted to briefly take a moment to

I choose to speak the words of my heart, for fear they will be lost in the confines of my mind, thus clouding my vision

express who I am today, because only then could you understand where I have been. I was ill yes, and I spent a year of my life in the confines of a cold hospital room strapped to machines, guzzling liquids through my nose.

"What a fun filled vacation," my forehead is presently wrinkled at my sense of humor, but you have to find laughter in your time of storm.

I found life, and the sense to live it. I used to ask the girls in my program, "What does the question, what will you be when you grow up mean to you?"

The answers were the obvious ones, doctor, lawyer, entertainer…, I was not amused. Very few of us actually become these childhood dream seekers. Life happens, and many of us lose our way because of the trials and tribulations.

So I changed the focus of this all too common question we throw our children's way. "What will you do when you grow up?" Good question! "Where will this life take you?" Sounds like an adventurous

I choose to speak the words of my heart, for fear they will be lost in the confines of my mind, thus clouding my vision

notion! How about this one? "What will you do with this life?" That one sounded like you are already destined to screw up.

The truth is, if you are already living and doing nothing then we have essentially already answered that question, **"LIVING PROOF THAT WE PLAN TO DO NOTHING!"**

Here is the new approach. "What will you do in death? What will you leave behind? What will your friends and family have to say about your character? How might they describe the way in which you *Lived* your life?"

To truly live we must have something to show for our time on earth. Our birth certificate is proof of our existence. Our resume is proof of our productivity. With a little fluff and finesse, the job is ours.

In death, I wrote journals of ways in which I wanted to live. I find that quite humorous, because we as humans experience travesty and then we are saved. We remember God and his promise. We fall

I choose to speak the words of my heart, for fear they will be lost in the confines of my mind, thus clouding my vision

to our knees praying for a second chance
and repentance of our sins, when this ritual
should have been daily. I thought for sure
my fear was death during my close walk
with it; but when I felt as if all was lost I
embraced it.

So began the cycle, fear of death
before success, and the fear of success for
fear of death. Now so close to achieving
dreams, you let go, afraid to fail, afraid of
responsibility, and afraid to follow through.

I spoke words of encouragement and
inspiration to staff of the hospital. When I
was able to walk, I visited other patients and
prayed at their bedside and kept them
company. I don't know today where that
loss of fear came from. I had a glow upon
me that couldn't be medically explained.

I wanted to fight and do something. I
wanted to prove that that old saying I yelled
while crossing the stage in high school. "IM
GONE BE FAMOUS YALL!"

I graduated, "Aija, I need a Butler."
It was true. I am never satisfied. I need
this... I want this.

*I choose to speak the words of my heart,
for fear they will be lost in the confines
of my mind, thus clouding my vision*

You may say greed. I say drive. If I am not satisfied with my current situation then I take steps to make a better one. Ten years ago I was fighting for my life. Today I have added the lives of my children. These children I was told I'd never have.

When I lie down in death I would like my children to know that their mother was a strong educated woman. A woman that did what she had to, to make a way for her children to grow and achieve respectably.

Nothing I do is for me. As a mother I am responsible for the lives of my offspring.

In death I want my friends and family to speak of good cheer. You ask how she lived, I ask how she died? Did she die with honor? Was her life led with love and respect, due diligence to succeed?

We will never be perfect. Our daily struggle is to become better productive individuals. Learn to use your life experiences to curb your will for good. It's easy to fail. It's easy to die. So take a

I choose to speak the words of my heart, for fear they will be lost in the confines of my mind, thus clouding my vision

moment to consider your eulogy. How
would you like it to read?

*I choose to speak the words of my heart,
for fear they will be lost in the confines
of my mind, thus clouding my vision*

I FOUND THE WILL TO LIVE IN MY DYING HOUR...

What does it truly mean to live in the moment? Is it to understand that this particular moment lives peace, understanding, joy, and truth of oneself?

There's often a moment when we cease to remember our dreams. There are times when we think, "What if?" We share many feelings of regret, when we do not seek the true aspirations of our heart. It is my time for self-fulfillment; I saved room for error. I developed patience in pursuing my goals. I let go of many dreams, only to put them into perspective. I decided to start and finish one goal at a time. I can't afford to quit. I won't! I shall finish my goal list, one by one, even if I finish last...

I choose to speak the words of my heart, for fear they will be lost in the confines of my mind, thus clouding my vision

I fear for those who do not have self-love. True happiness cannot be sought within the minds of others. I pity those who do not seek truth within themselves. It becomes boring and uneventful to live someone else's dream. Choose you, you may become conformed, enriched by environment; but speak with the opinions of thy own.

Sometimes we reflect on the child within. The child which was never afraid of taking risks ventured spontaneously without a second glance or ponders of consequence, all our hopes seen in the clearest of views. Sadly, in years to come, and in moments of the present we get a false start, then we give up all together.

There are always choices that must be made. Right and wrong exists in your own conscience. Life is a challenge... The survival of the fittest...

I give you formal consent. The consent to act on the things you believe in,

I choose to speak the words of my heart, for fear they will be lost in the confines of my mind, thus clouding my vision

and encourage others to do the same. Before I came to understand my options and the business of re-organizing my life and its changes, my space on earth was disheveled. It took a life and death situation for me to put things into perspective.

A part of me died, in the confines of a cold hospital room; but when I reached the time of my release, I was reborn. This is the beginning, my moment of truth, my time.

I choose to speak the words of my heart, for fear they will be lost in the confines of my mind, thus clouding my vision

TAKING RESPONSIBILITY FOR YOUR OWN ACTIONS

Be encouraged, it is easy to flee from your responsibility. For added responsibility begets organization, productivity, thus success. So remember right or wrong, take responsibility for your own actions. Guaranteed, if you steal something you and only you, will be imprisoned. Not those who may have dared you to do so.

I choose to speak the words of my heart, for fear they will be lost in the confines of my mind, thus clouding my vision

SPIRITUAL GUIDANCE AND PRAYER

Late night devotion begins with my writing to the sound of the fans hum, I reflect on the day's events. My time of self-counsel allows me to adjust my attitude, calm my state of mind, and repent for my sins. I thank God for giving me the insight to see and correct my faults.

I choose to speak the words of my heart, for fear they will be lost in the confines of my mind, thus clouding my vision

THE GOLDEN TICKET

Your NAME is essentially all that you have. Keep it clean, and in good standing. It will take you far.

I choose to speak the words of my heart, for fear they will be lost in the confines of my mind, thus clouding my vision

AIJA M. BUTLER

PAT YOURSELF ON THE BACK...

"The Team of Me," was a great concept. It was a Martin Lawrence film entitled, "Welcome Home Roscoe."

However in my version of the story, "The Team of me," is about correcting ones faults. This team works to acknowledge wrong doing, while listening to constructive criticism and taking heed.

My vision shows the team, (self), and the conscience working to tune his or her own attitude.

You work to refine yourself, into a better, stronger, respectable being. Thus, succeeding and earning your badge in congeniality.

I choose to speak the words of my heart, for fear they will be lost in the confines of my mind, thus clouding my vision

I AM AT WAR

I am… stepping high through the trenches.

I am at war. Daily I look my nemesis in the face and I wage war upon her doubtful slurs. She second guess' my work, she spits upon my efforts. I sometimes lose focus because of her evil deeds, but I reach within my bag of tricks and I win the fight. My reflection at times tells lies.

My reflection reveals the scars of my disease. They scream at the realities that one day I may be faced with once again. I cringe at those thoughts. Thoughts of defeat, I fear that If I had to revisit my times of great pain, I could not endure the same bout and my fate would result in total demise. I call out to my adversary, my nemesis screams and pulls my hair. I say to her that she could not beat me, for I am strong.

I choose to speak the words of my heart, for fear they will be lost in the confines of my mind, thus clouding my vision

I am a survivor. She says that the war is not over. Just because I have won the fight does not mean the wraths of this life are not upon me.

"I choose to stand" I say to her, this reflection in the mirror. If I were to flee, then I leave the decisions of this proclaimed life to circumstance. I don't want to be left behind because I was too cowardice to participate.

I'd much rather take my place. My reflection sometimes speaks ill of our journey. She threatens to change our venue with her slanderous talk. I look her dead on and I repeat these words,

"The war is on. The war is on. These are my scars, this is my life and I will fight to the finish, as sure as the day I was born..."

I choose to speak the words of my heart, for fear they will be lost in the confines of my mind, thus clouding my vision

AIJA M. BUTLER

THE DEFINITION OF A TRUE FRIEND

Trust and loyalty are the two main ingredients for long-lasting relationships. If I am to be called your friend, then I am a trustworthy person. I am respectful of your wishes. My lips are sealed unless granted permission to express our secrets. I am willing to be honest of your faults, shortcomings, and success'.

I choose to speak the words of my heart, for fear they will be lost in the confines of my mind, thus clouding my vision

AIJA M. BUTLER

FRIENDS AND FAMILY

Relationships are much like jobs.
You have to work hard to sustain them.

I choose to speak the words of my heart,
for fear they will be lost in the confines
of my mind, thus clouding my vision

AIJA M. BUTLER

MAKING WISE CHOICES AND HEALTHY BONDS

Do your best to mend fences that are broken. You never know when you may need a helping hand. However, if things are not broken, don't attempt to fix them. We must remember to stay humble as we venture to greener pastures. Those we cross on the way up are the same faces we meet on the way down. So grab a hammer and some paint, choose your color fence, just be sure it can weather the storm.

I choose to speak the words of my heart, for fear they will be lost in the confines of my mind, thus clouding my vision

UNDERSTANDING, COMPROMISE, AND RESPECT

Sadly love can't solve all of your issues. There must be a plan of action and implementation, much like an organized goal in a business plan.

If both parties are not on the same page there will be conflict?

Without communication there can't be a resolution. A partnership involves you as an individual; but it does not revolve around you.

There is no, "I," in team as the old saying goes. Don't confuse the "Team of me," notion with self-confidence and direction. This involves the conjoining of two individuals, with like goals and

I choose to speak the words of my heart, for fear they will be lost in the confines of my mind, thus clouding my vision

aspirations, whether it family, business, or intimacy.

We tend to forget that often. It is easy to start pointing the finger, especially when we feel that we have been wronged or misunderstood. First message to take a mental note of, communication IS key!

Without understanding, compromise, and respect for one another's feelings, you will never experience loves joy. When in fact you have come to a compromise, the decision made between all parties may end in a separation of the heart.

Remember to use words of encouragement and express them to your partner readily.

I choose to speak the words of my heart, for fear they will be lost in the confines of my mind, thus clouding my vision

AIJA M. BUTLER

WHAT'S YOUR WORTH

Cherish what you have. If what you have is worth mentioning? In times of indifference, the grass may seem greener in another pasture. You must be sure to remember that only a real man can know a woman's worth, If you can be considered a woman yourself?

I choose to speak the words of my heart, for fear they will be lost in the confines of my mind, thus clouding my vision

SAY WHAT YOU MEAN, DO WHAT YOU SAY

If you say that you are going to do something, it is important to stay true to your word. This is true especially when dealing with business partners, and funny as it may sound children. Children rarely forget a promise and they are likely to call you on it in a public setting.

If the promises you enlist can't be kept due to unforeseen forces of life, take the time to explain yourself. Life happens, and people are most understanding of that fact, just as long as they are told the truth in advance.

I choose to speak the words of my heart, for fear they will be lost in the confines of my mind, thus clouding my vision

AIJA M. BUTLER

SPONTANEOUS OR JUST STUPID

Do you plan for the unexpected or allow the unexpected to call the shots? It's one thing to be spontaneous in ventures that won't affect your social stature or the economics of your household. It's another to just be reckless and irresponsible.

I choose to speak the words of my heart, for fear they will be lost in the confines of my mind, thus clouding my vision

COPPING OUT, PLANNING= CHANGE

I have come to find that planning is essential to successfully completing tasks. Sometimes the unexpected snag will delay a project's completion; but those delays should never result in a dream deferred.

Usually when we become frustrated with the obstacles set before us, we fail to realize that with planning comes change. We need to prepare for the change as new plans develop. They go hand in hand.

I choose to speak the words of my heart, for fear they will be lost in the confines of my mind, thus clouding my vision

GO GETTER!

Be sure to plan ahead. I can't say this enough. Matter of fact, this exact statement should be mentioned after every three pages of this book. Just to remind readers of the importance of having your own back.

Sometimes we get comfortable and start relying on either other sources, or people to cover our ass.

Whereas, if you handle business affairs appropriately you will succeed in goal, planning, and implementation; In order to get ahead you must be smarter than the average bear.

Aye...Yogi

I choose to speak the words of my heart, for fear they will be lost in the confines of my mind, thus clouding my vision

CRITICAL THINKING

SETTING THE PACE FOR SUCCESS

Never make promises you can't keep. Do not accept a multitude of tasks. You will become overwhelmed with stress; and the inability to complete tasks adequately.

I choose to speak the words of my heart, for fear they will be lost in the confines of my mind, thus clouding my vision

THE REBIRTH OF MY SOUL, 2ND EDITION

AIJA M. BUTLER

*I choose to speak the words of my heart,
for fear they will be lost in the confines
of my mind, thus clouding my vision*

FIGHT TO THE FINISH FALL DOWN 7 TIMES GET UP 8

The life of a true visionary has its perks in the end, but it takes extreme hard work and dedication. Do you have a vision for your life? Are you working towards your ultimate goal, in terms of financial stability? Life happens and it becomes a huge trial to overcome some mistakes.

Though, if you have a vision and the dedication to make those aspirations a reality; the trials and tribulations become stepping stones to a bigger and brighter future.

I choose to speak the words of my heart, for fear they will be lost in the confines of my mind, thus clouding my vision

GOOD VS. EVIL, THE BATTLE OF THE CONSCIOUSNESS

The trials of your life can cause you to experience loss of rational thought. Stifle those unconscious views of the "ID" personality.

It is jealous and never satisfied. You will fall prey to the demons of your mind. The villains lay dormant by the superego, which allows us to decipher right and wrong.

I choose to speak the words of my heart, for fear they will be lost in the confines of my mind, thus clouding my vision

JEALOUSY

Jealousy can fuel a murderous rage and cause actions that are far beyond necessary. If your heart tends to wander towards another's demise, in light of their blessings, this may poison your mind and ruin your own path to success.

Check yourself! Congratulate, don't hate! To whom all blessings flow.

I choose to speak the words of my heart, for fear they will be lost in the confines of my mind, thus clouding my vision

NURTURE AND DEVELOPMENT

Children are creative, artistic souls that need guidance. Creativity can make you a star. It can also be a deal breaker if not properly cultivated. We must teach our youth to dream big, but realistically.

I choose to speak the words of my heart, for fear they will be lost in the confines of my mind, thus clouding my vision

LIFE CHOICES

It's hard to stand alone. The egg upon your face stifles the road to independence. Flinging your self-confidence towards an abyss of nothingness in the land of social demands; but standing for what you believe in is a great way to establish credibility. The minority of the conforming majority is a tough pill to swallow.

Still, be encouraged. Establish values and belief systems you are willing to stand by. You will be tested.

I choose to speak the words of my heart, for fear they will be lost in the confines of my mind, thus clouding my vision

I MADE A LIST...

My list contained projects I would like to either endorse or develop. It also contained courses I needed to take to acquire the appropriate credentials to facilitate such an endeavor.

My list was then split into 3 parts. The first section highlighted my goals, and a desired time frame to complete those goals.

The second section contained goals that could be considered short term goals. For example, the actual plan in itself is a short term goal. You must first develop a plan of action before you can start to work on the goals on your list.

The third section consisted of long term goals. Such as what you expect to be doing, say 3-5 years down the line, once you have developed and completed the training for your desired career or program's development. It's very much like asking. **"What do I want to be when I grow up?"**

I choose to speak the words of my heart, for fear they will be lost in the confines of my mind, thus clouding my vision

If you have completed the task of goal set-up, it is now time to map out your goal implementation. How are you going to achieve these goals? More so, when does this plan of action begin, and realistically considering all facets of life, when will this said goal, be complete?

Now during the plan of action stage you must consider a few things before setting a timeline:

1. You need to consider your **study habits.** Are you disciplined, does it take you a little longer to retain information?

2. Time management. Many of us are returning to school or continuing education while developing our families. Realistically we need to look at our daily schedules to determine what would be a good time to attend classes or work etc., especially for those that are single parents or have small children.

3. Lastly, the **workforce and forecast** for the job or career you are pursuing. Have you done your research? Is there a need for

I choose to speak the words of my heart, for fear they will be lost in the confines of my mind, thus clouding my vision

specialists in which ever field you are interested in going into?

Once you have completed these tasks you can rationally, map out your tour to success.

CONFIDENCE

IN LOVE AND RESPECT

Confidence: The feeling or belief that one can rely on someone or something; firm trust: "we had every **confidence in** our love, in one another," The state of feeling certain about the truth of something. "He is the truth, He is ready for love."

Faith: Complete trust or confidence in someone or something. If I am confident in him I am faithful

The cycle has restarted and I am faced with the two issues that seem to plague my journey with recovery.

The words sickly are etched into my cerebral cortex and its singes the nerves in my feet and hands. They burn when I try to step towards positive venue. My fingers grow weary and cramp up when I raise my hands towards the sky or reach for a pen.

I choose to speak the words of my heart, for fear they will be lost in the confines of my mind, thus clouding my vision

My goals become tarnished old and worn pieces of brass. The smell of defeat hover's me. I am cooled by my contempt and rather confident in my ability to drop the ball.

"Oh ye of little faith," This man of God told me.

This love that was greater than any love a human could possibly possess so I often checked his pulse and bit into his flesh to see if his blood was as red as mine. I imagined in light his skin would take the look of diamonds sparkling under the sun's light.

This love I often dreamed of…unconditional and one that resembled that of God. You see the love that God has for his children has no boundaries. Much like the mental connection I found in this physical being of human perfection. Not perfect as in fault…perfect in that with those faults brought forth the appreciation of those pleasurable characteristics that are surely never to be taken granted of.

This Rebirth moment is brought to you by a blossoming rose. It's blossoming, taking its full color and form, its thorns

I choose to speak the words of my heart, for fear they will be lost in the confines of my mind, thus clouding my vision

sharp and blood thirsty, confident. Now, reborn this rose is showered with all that it is needed to survive, the water and sun, and the faith that the well will never run dry.

I woke up in cold sweat, his smell lingering in the dark like smoke from a lit cigar. I sat up quickly but my eyes remained closed. I needed to feel his presence but my eyes wouldn't part; I couldn't let my mind turn my thoughts of him to form a physical presence. In case he was still far-away. I grabbed hold of the corner of my nightstand. The lump in my throat formed. And my hands shook as I reached out to the now cold room. My limbs went numb and ice froze my tears. My lips now meld together by the fear of coming to terms, closure, death of my hero, my medals of honor boxed and shining through the dark.

I cursed him… prying my lips apart with my hot breath…,

"Your obligation is to me," I screamed at his shadow one I knew was there. I yelled and asked why. My guts were soft I felt nauseated and a sense of the plague. My

I choose to speak the words of my heart, for fear they will be lost in the confines of my mind, thus clouding my vision

body was so cold it felt like he was attempting to freeze me to death.

"Stop," is all I heard…the whisper in the dark.

The warning of my negative tone was reprimanded before I could go deep to hurt my own confidence. Why I called back into the darkness, then said just come home. You are so far away. I'm dying without you baby.

Let my fears rest come and lay with me. Melt me with your kiss. Argue with me to make the make-up sex that much better. Take me into your arms and let me know that you are ok and will never leave me alone again.

Tell me you love me, tell me you want me, tell me you need me…As my nights turn into weeks of loneliness I sit and think of you. Showers no longer help. My thoughts plague me in the steam. You haunt my dreams, my thoughts my world.

I see you come to me. Love me. Let me love you…

I choose to speak the words of my heart, for fear they will be lost in the confines of my mind, thus clouding my vision

ALL CHOKED UP

IN AND OUT OF LOVE, RECOVERY
IN OF IT'S OWN

AROUND AGAIN...

Today I inhaled smoke. I was choked up and the air caught into my lungs. I never exhaled. I was sifting through old pictures wondering where the time had gone. My hands were bent out of shape and my back now worn. My years were still young but my heart was old and torn.

The scars of my flesh tore through my self-confidence like 30 mile an hour winds through a rose garden.

Saved by the remnants of love brought life into my willowing limbs, though my speech slurred by brains default it was no bother.

I choose to speak the words of my heart, for fear they will be lost in the confines of my mind, thus clouding my vision

AIJA M. BUTLER

My fear of success gave him chase. He stood right there cheering me on and coaching me ensuring that there was no time to waste.

Dreamy it became this fantasy being that he had taken the place of medication.

Life happens...my tears begin to flow...God receives a direct hit from me...I question his will because for this I just have to know...

Loves wrath left a horrific mark. The "X" burned into my flesh and continued to smoke well into the night.

Huffing and puffing at this wound that didn't seem to heal more less settle from its initial singe kept me up at night. I rocked frantically in worry and in fear. Longing no matter who phoned his voice I had to hear...now calm but still unease I sit and write these words...

it is well into my day 365 where my journey has to end...but this life of love, illness, and recovery continues as my strong limbs*sigh...continue to bend.

I choose to speak the words of my heart, for fear they will be lost in the confines of my mind, thus clouding my vision

REHAB...

Life can be as good and fulfilling as you make it.

There are an abundance of mistakes to be made. It is how you recover from those shortcomings that will determine your place in line.

We live and **should** learn from our life experiences.

What will be your resolution? Your answer is detrimental to the acute or chronic illness of the mind. What will be your rise and fall? When YOU get knocked down, HOW do you recover?

"Fall down 8 times, getup 9, I say."

Would you believe that our biggest enemy can easily be ourselves, simply by second guessing our ability to achieve greatness?

That is a serious issue. I call it, "The

I choose to speak the words of my heart, for fear they will be lost in the confines of my mind, thus clouding my vision

diseased mind."

We have enough haters within our own circles to deal with more or less, our own insecurities.

Consider rehab, a rehabilitation of the mind, in the way that we approach failures, mistakes, and misfortune.

We can recover from any down fall as long as we are certain of our abilities to succeed.

So again I say, "Fall down 8 times, getup 9."

I choose to speak the words of my heart, for fear they will be lost in the confines of my mind, thus clouding my vision

AIJA M. BUTLER

9/11...

There are times during my day, when I happen to glance at the clock and notice the time. Periodically it reads 9:11. I panic every time. I immediately feel a sense of horrific pain in the pit of my stomach. Something horrible is going to happen. I believe the date to be plagued with misfortune, of any scale. I am usually not superstitious. However, this date was such a horrific day that any form of the numbers drew me to tears. My stomach drops and I start to hyperventilate.

Often times when the clock strikes 9:11..., I wait. I struggle to pull myself from bed. If I am busy in work, school, home or play, I stop to ponder an escape. God forbid another tragedy like 9/11 takes place.

How could you honestly prepare? Could the world? How do you foresee a plan to escape the unknown? My fight continues to shake my feelings of anxiety.

I choose to speak the words of my heart, for fear they will be lost in the confines of my mind, thus clouding my vision

I am living, a life engulfed in fear. Don't make the choice to fear the unknown. If you do you will become lost in suspended animation. Unable to move, progress, and therefore, succeed… Prepare in ways to continue your enrichment of the soul. 9/11 may or may not come around again, but there will be many forms of 9/11 in your individual lives.

Don't let the fear of those misfortunes stop you from living your life to the fullest.

I choose to speak the words of my heart, for fear they will be lost in the confines of my mind, thus clouding my vision

AFTER THE STORM...

After the storm the clouds lightened to a pearl white. The rain left puddles of water and wet leaves. It was clear and quiet outside my window. The soft knock of the rain had gone. I came from under my soft blanket. I took refuge shielding myself from the angry storm.

Still, the thunderous rage, drummed outside my wall, until the storm's end. The thunder no longer threatened to take my soul. It slithered away cowardly. The wind stopped screaming at my window. Branches from the winds rage were scattered upon the ground.

They died during winds wrath, separating from their roots, a disastrous but necessary event of nature.

Life after the storm is much like the quiet just before the storm hits. We don't

I choose to speak the words of my heart, for fear they will be lost in the confines of my mind, thus clouding my vision

know how hard it will hit or what kind of damage our earthly possessions will sustain, but there is no running from it. Life happens, in scenes. Like a movie it jumps back and forth from character to character.

Life's changing adventures take place and we don't know where and when or how bad or good the outcome will be. However, we must continue to roll with the punches.

I choose to speak the words of my heart, for fear they will be lost in the confines of my mind, thus clouding my vision

AUXILIARY LABELS PROCEED WITH CAUTION...

It is in my professional opinion that situations of life should be recorded and filed accordingly. People should be labeled with the appropriate auxiliary labels. Prescription medications are mandated to disclose potential dangers and side effects to their use. Why not do the same for real life situations?

We should have warning signs on people, businesses, eateries, and the list goes on. Simple imbedded fluorescent warning labels that light up upon introduction.

"Hi my name is Aija, overly sensitive workaholic." Wow did I say that? Well honesty sure beats trying to hide the true components of your personality. If you know what I bring to the table, maybe, just

I choose to speak the words of my heart, for fear they will be lost in the confines of my mind, thus clouding my vision

maybe you will be able to handle situations appropriately.

Some of you may not be too fond of the auxiliary labels, you so deserve. Just in case any of these bright ideas I am sure to have patented come to pass. I would think long and hard about changing some of those nasty bad habits we carry around in our pockets.

I choose to speak the words of my heart, for fear they will be lost in the confines of my mind, thus clouding my vision

STRIVING FOR SUCCESS

My dreams are of success and love, in this life. Daily I strive to push forward and persevere

I choose to speak the words of my heart, for fear they will be lost in the confines of my mind, thus clouding my vision

WANT TO MAKE A BET?

Gambling is a tricky sport and it can be very addicting.

With one win you are convinced that your luck is here to stay and it will never run out.

Why gamble for mere pennies. The true tricks of the trade come from those which use their God given talents. The noodle, your brain rather.

Stop wasting your chips on bets you have no control over. Those funds you are using to place your bets could be used to buy diapers, wipes, food etc.

You can bet your life on success. The ball is always in your court. You just need to step your game up and decide just whose team you are on.

I choose to speak the words of my heart, for fear they will be lost in the confines of my mind, thus clouding my vision

AIJA M. BUTLER

So! Who do you play for?
ITS GAME TIME...

*I choose to speak the words of my heart,
for fear they will be lost in the confines
of my mind, thus clouding my vision*

ODE' TO LOVE

I wanted to say goodbye, but love wouldn't let me go;

In the middle of the night I crept softly, packing a small bag, but love wouldn't let me flee;

Although my heart is full of love, my mind and body had grown tired, I sought a calm and relaxing getaway.

The duties were overwhelming, and the hours of the day are too few.

Juggling my career and family gets overwhelming at times;

But as the children's laughs and screams entered my dreams, love wouldn't let me leave.

I sift through the pages of my diary, to share a small segment of this love story.

I choose to speak the words of my heart, for fear they will be lost in the confines of my mind, thus clouding my vision

AIJA M. BUTLER

My Family is of high importance;
Order is another;

Sometimes order gets in the way of
my two rambunctious boys, and high
maintenance fashion addicted, daughter.
Hence, Loves Joy beckons me to stay.

My bag remains packed deep within
the depths of my closet;

But love can't seem to let me
retrieve it.

My away bag is on standby.
Packing and unpacking is my form of
counsel.

I am tired always. And in a cleaning
frenzy, I could easily throw the dirty laundry
away.

I would love to sleep in, in the
morning.

To possibly sleep the stress away.

Lately, almost always my dreams
and goals get in the way; but yet and still,

*I choose to speak the words of my heart,
for fear they will be lost in the confines
of my mind, thus clouding my vision*

love won't let go.

Instead I believe, love may be my muse.

My way of focus.

My support system, I'd have to say.

Without this love, it may be quite easy to stray,

This love that often hurts but beckons me to stay.

I choose to speak the words of my heart, for fear they will be lost in the confines of my mind, thus clouding my vision

MIND OVER MATTER

Our goals are our success. Our
failures are the result of our fears.

*I choose to speak the words of my heart,
for fear they will be lost in the confines
of my mind, thus clouding my vision*

FRIENDS AND FAMILY

Relationships are much like jobs.
You have to work hard to sustain them.

*I choose to speak the words of my heart,
for fear they will be lost in the confines
of my mind, thus clouding my vision*

EXILED

I stomped in and slammed the door, and I headed straight upstairs. They were having one of their sessions. You know the ones where you can hear all the loud talk and laughter yards away, but when your presence is shown all is quiet. I cut my eyes and kept going on my way. I wasn't in the mood for games. It doesn't take a brain surgeon to notice when your name is the topic of a conversation. I wasn't at all surprised. I was used to the deception.

Myself, and other females are like viruses. I never seem to have much in common with other women except our boobs and vaginas. I'm not interested in shopping all times of day and night or gossiping for more than 20 minutes at a time. If my husband hasn't either called or come home on time, I don't run and jump into my vehicle in search of him or his fair companion.

This assumption does not speak for

I choose to speak the words of my heart, for fear they will be lost in the confines of my mind, thus clouding my vision

all women. It does, however, weigh heavily on my bouts with those I have personally had dealings.

So, how did I decide to deal with the small talk the women of my purse club conducted without my presence?

Simple, I withdrew my membership and cancelled my most recent patronage to the association.

It was a lost cause. I needed a break from drama anyhow. I'd had enough of others butting their noses in my affairs contributing nothing, but more problems for me to deal with. I stumped on my membership badge and threw away the complimentary coffee cup. I saw them retrieve it from an old dusty box from the back of their supply closet, anyhow.

Some invitation! I curtsied after dumping the shattered glass onto the living room coffee table and ripped up my recent dues check.

The looks on their faces was priceless. They played me but, I got the last

I choose to speak the words of my heart, for fear they will be lost in the confines of my mind, thus clouding my vision

laugh. There was no way I would continue to play the 3rd wheel, the gal with the open purse.

The highly educated but gullible as hell, many of us have played this role in our groups of girlfriends and or associates. The difference I've learned in the matter of forming bonds with women is simple. We are already emotional creatures. We are naturally competitive by way of societal influence. I find that the women I don't get along with, tend to have issues within themselves. I learned that I could have beautiful relationships with other women without the drama. I learned that it's not that I don't like women, they don't like themselves.

This, breeds, jealousy, deception, and maliciousness. An old saying comes to mind as I write this passage. Misery loves company. I too, was one of those unhappy creatures, just waiting for the target to arrive at our gossip girl tea party. She never knew she was the topic, of the group's evil plan to demean her self-esteem.

We all were targets at some point

I choose to speak the words of my heart, for fear they will be lost in the confines of my mind, thus clouding my vision

and time. If I could stand not being a part of an elite group at the time, I would have fled just before my turn to feel the wrath of my coconspirators. My low self-esteem was only growing as I paid honorable mention to those I felt were beneath me.

You ever notice friends or associates that tend to always want to discuss the issues of another? Nothing in their personal lives seems to be of any importance. They never have news to share of their own. They are in waiting to see who they may bash and belittle, brightening their own day if only for a moment.

Acceptance can be a serious issue, with not only those in adolescence. We may continue to do things that are not of our personal nature, well into adulthood. This sometimes has very little to do with maturity. We may mature into productive adults with responsibilities that we take care of, however, this doesn't make us respectable human beings. These traits have to do with the respect and esteem we have for ourselves.

How can we proclaim to value

I choose to speak the words of my heart, for fear they will be lost in the confines of my mind, thus clouding my vision

AIJA M. BUTLER

another if we do not hold or carry ourselves at a level of respectability?

I encourage those of you with who, carry these she devil traits, to ditch the act and start loving on yourselves, faults, flaws, and failures. Only then can you begin to be the best person you can be.

I choose to speak the words of my heart, for fear they will be lost in the confines of my mind, thus clouding my vision

AIJA M. BUTLER

WALKING BUT CAN'T RUN JUST YET...

I heard you sneaking about your haven, your mind now confused and disheveled. The first set of goals and circumstance seemed to cure itself with little or no effort from you. It has been an easy road to recovery thus far. Only now, your name has been called. It's time for you to prove your case. Now you are nervous and want to hide among the many heads in a crowd.

You don't do so well with the word, "No." It's not as easy to swallow when everything you ask for has been granted without question. You have to work a little harder now and you don't know if you are up for the challenge. Well it won't be easy, and your tour to success isn't always going to be peaches and cream.

It's time to strap down and fasten

I choose to speak the words of my heart, for fear they will be lost in the confines of my mind, thus clouding my vision

your seat belts and prepare for a long ride.

I've learned that with any goal or plan, there is a journey that comes along with execution. Life happens! We must be willing and able to sway with the winds. The storms are going to come, but they will also pass. So let's not just throw in our towels when things get rough.

"Not so fast," I like to say to myself, when I feel the urge to simply give in.

There are many battles in this war we call, "Life."

I choose to speak the words of my heart, for fear they will be lost in the confines of my mind, thus clouding my vision

DIE HARD FAN OF ME

Ok, we can argue all day about this but, I'm famous.

Now, I know this may be the first time you have heard my name. But yes this is true; I'm famous.

The Team of Me is in highlights and my Coach Purse is authentic.

I have a job and an education which continues to flourish. I have accomplished many endeavors, and look to add many more to my resume.

I understand the hullabaloo, about actors and actresses, music entertainers, and the like.

However, I love music, television, etc. But I don't have time to glorify there success'.

I choose to speak the words of my heart, for fear they will be lost in the confines of my mind, thus clouding my vision

If I utilize all my time discussing tabloids and others livelihoods, how is this going to get me ahead.

Don't get me wrong I can appreciate an example, a guide, or even tools to learn how to hustle.

But I got to spend my time cheering me on. Like I said I'm famous in my eyes. I don't even sign autographs because it takes time away from my life's work.

You ever attend a concert where ladies are literally passing out because of a musical artist? Can you believe that chicks throw their underwear at celebrity's.

Ladies, you may want to keep those drawls. If you continue to spend so much time worshiping others you may miss out on your own opportunities.

You must understand that they too, work hard for their money. You must be present and on top of your game as well.

Appreciate but don't worship. Make

I choose to speak the words of my heart, for fear they will be lost in the confines of my mind, thus clouding my vision

use of that energy for your own fans.

I choose to speak the words of my heart,
for fear they will be lost in the confines
of my mind, thus clouding my vision

BACK SEAT DRIVING

In life you should be the driver of your own vehicle. Many of us are stuck in the back seat and allowing circumstance to drive us around. As we all know, you can't tell other folk how to drive, or where to go. Even taxi cabs take their own route.

Stop wasting your gas on worthless trips. Spending countless hours, rolling up and down the same block. Tour a new venue. Repossess your car from the ways of this world. We need to drive our own shit. Fast and Furiously!

I choose to speak the words of my heart, for fear they will be lost in the confines of my mind, thus clouding my vision

BUSTED AND DISGUSTED

Sometimes I feel like I am moving in slow motion. There are other times when I feel as if I am not moving at all. The peak of planning is underway and the waiting game begins. I become bored and at times I lose sight of my goals. Half way through I start to doubt myself.

This is a pet peeve of mine, one of many I wage war upon daily. On this progressive road to understanding, I purge feelings of ambiguity. I vow to suppress the devils advances to steal away my life's treasures.

When in doubt, my wheels start to turn. I have thoughts of fear and discomfort. Depression settles and I am overcome with sleep.

Lately, I am learning to revisit my goal sheet. It is displayed in a frame as if it

I choose to speak the words of my heart, for fear they will be lost in the confines of my mind, thus clouding my vision

is a fine work of art. I refocus my train of thought, and embrace the down time to relieve stress.

I am continuous in learning what working under stress does to the human body, and the difference between working well under stress and being a stressed individual.

Working while stressed does not mean that you are working hard or up to par. It could simply suggest that you are not working with a full deck.

Working well under stress and working while stressed is two different things. You don't have to have a pile of work waiting for you to consider yourself busy or accomplished. This all goes back to my schedule day planner and PDA, have we gotten that far yet. No we haven't but be sure to read, "Message Board!" That passage will say it all.

I am quite surprised at myself as I am learning how to be successful and maintain it. I hope that you too, have been listening and highlighting this book.

I choose to speak the words of my heart, for fear they will be lost in the confines of my mind, thus clouding my vision

AIJA M. BUTLER

Now that we know how to plan, time management, and the hoopla about the reality of security, our cups should be half full. For ladies and gentlemen, I will not rest until we have been replenished.

I choose to speak the words of my heart, for fear they will be lost in the confines of my mind, thus clouding my vision

LOVE YOUR NEIGHBOR

Be careful to treat others in the way you would want to be treated. Often times when we are wronged we let our emotions over-ride reason.

When you forget to take others feelings into consideration, you ruin relationships with colleagues, family members, and friends.

Thus, burning bridges you may later need to cross.

I choose to speak the words of my heart, for fear they will be lost in the confines of my mind, thus clouding my vision

LOSS OF RATIONAL THOUGHT

Love was unlocked in my mind's eye and I was desperate to retrieve it. I am a refined individual, lost at one point in the realm of lust and greed. Notice, there was no love there. The focus was to get ahead. Survival of the fittest… Doesn't the measure of material wealth showcase your social status? Is money not the race? This is what this whole life thing is about, right? Who I can screw before I myself became the recipient of the ass fuck, without lubrication. So I drift…I use my long lifetime of bad company to justify my new improved way of living. I become the attacker. I am tired of being the gum beneath ones feet, desperately trying to hold on to the possibility of being accepted. Long is the awaited drowse of horrific depression. I sulk…and I slither…I

I choose to speak the words of my heart, for fear they will be lost in the confines of my mind, thus clouding my vision

swore to spectators that I was a well-known
scholar and how dare they spit upon my
countenance as though my thoughts weren't
pertinent. I wept…I slid upon the cold floors
of a drab tiled public restroom. The stench
of piss dried my nasal passage and forced
me to breathe from my mouth, inhaling the
toxins. There it happened. Disease riddled
my lungs, filtered my being and tore my
heart and soul. Once placed in total demise
status just seconds before death, a light
appeared in the fold of my room's darkened
blinds; and my eyes were forced to close.
Insightful this moment…as I looked to seek
justice for this poor unfortunate event.

I was given the opportunity to live.
Still, enraged by past dark moons, I fell
short of motivation. I was found slumped
over with my hands inappropriately placed
as if caught while masturbating. Awaken my
shocked eyes I claimed to have lost my
mind…placed on meds…I'd managed to
buy sometime.

*I choose to speak the words of my heart,
for fear they will be lost in the confines
of my mind, thus clouding my vision*

AIJA M. BUTLER

This new love I'd walked into was like a damn brick wall. Too high for me to climb so at one point I figured I would just go around. This life after a moment of peace and tranquility is forging dangerously towards chaos. The emotion of love's whirlwind is overriding reason…

I choose to speak the words of my heart, for fear they will be lost in the confines of my mind, thus clouding my vision

SCAR TISSUE

I have these scars. I cover them with make-up. They still shine through. My section of the world is tarnished and plagued with the idea of early demise. Sitting staring out of the window now...each day that passes I wither away. From the cold confines of this hospital room I imagine the smell of fresh air. I envision my feet touching grass. Although, afraid the inhalation air outside my protective bubble will kill me. I am stranded in the notion that I may survive. I know however the DNR has been signed. My head hurts, my legs ache but still I smile. My father's at my feet and he sobs quietly....He doesn't know that I know. I pretend to sleep. In hopes for a silent and lonely death, don't think I could let go if my daughter was around. I'd hang on to every dying breath as the pain stabbed from my chest to my toes.

I choose to speak the words of my heart, for fear they will be lost in the confines of my mind, thus clouding my vision

Secretly I would beg for my spectators to leave. Let me drift off cowardly alone and in slumber. I watch as the nurse's wheel yet another soul that has gone home down the hall. White sheets white as snow, steel frame lain under its crisp linen. My journal's full…my nurse button flashes.

In comes the staff on cue. There only job is to provide comfort. Meds…none presently…I need a journal and a pack of 10 pens. The nurse obliged. She returned in good timing and my thoughts out poured. The letter to my daughter spoke of my wants and well wishes. The letter to my mother forgave her, the letter to my father I understand, the letter to my siblings do you and never stop.

I choose to speak the words of my heart, for fear they will be lost in the confines of my mind, thus clouding my vision

BURN BRIGHT

In the midst of darkness there is still light. The candle burning within can pull you ashore. Believe in yourself. Trust in you, have faith.

I choose to speak the words of my heart, for fear they will be lost in the confines of my mind, thus clouding my vision

AIJA M. BUTLER

WRITING IS MY MUSE

Sometimes my only comfort is that this disease has yet to take over my brain. My speech is sometimes slurred and my words get lost in the winds when voiced, but my pen still writes earnestly until my well runs dry. The anxiety of it all is unsettling. I often panic and have ill feelings of the future.

"What if…," often lies in the confines of my mind? Thoughts of positive thought are often drowned by the realities of disease. The aches and pains override hope. My faith is often tested after the prognosis. My head pounds, my eyesight becomes blurry and I am filled with self-doubt. It is one of these days where I have to sift through the madness of it all to get back to my transformation. The night sweats of 2003 haunt me. The medicine cabinet at my

I choose to speak the words of my heart, for fear they will be lost in the confines of my mind, thus clouding my vision

bed side cripples me. I am found, out cold, once again…saddened and awakened by disease. I write so I can remember my story. I can never tell if my words will slip from under me during the night. I sometimes awake and words that are common knowledge are a blur to me. The frustration sickens me. My loss of hope drowns me. It's these days when I grab hold of God's unchanging hand and I pray for strength. Only then can I truly walk in faith. His footprints in the sand right next to me.

Writing my thoughts down earnestly to rid my soul of ill feelings going through the many stages of death and dying…

I choose to speak the words of my heart, for fear they will be lost in the confines of my mind, thus clouding my vision

AIJA M. BUTLER

REJUVENATION 2X

Tackling my faults bringing light to my short comings, I am standing in a new light. My words are refined as my speech is no longer slurred. My skin has been washed clean is milk and honey. I have repented for my sins and I AM NOT AFRAID.

I choose to speak the words of my heart, for fear they will be lost in the confines of my mind, thus clouding my vision

AIJA M. BUTLER

WHAT A JERK

A *Jerk* is someone that is completely out of to lunch on all subject matters. I know a few, quite well and thought to share this bit of advice to those with who may come in close contact with this bunch.

Well, at first, we must be aware of the type of personality we are dealing with. These individuals have little or no concern for others, personal life, issues or to do list. They willingly interrupt your schedule on a whim and will continue to dial and text your phone inquiring about your schedule and when you will be able to assist them in their endeavors.

They have no respect for themselves and seem to lack the emotions of embarrassment and remorse. However, they appear to be hurt when others wash their hands of them or have had enough of their indecent behaviors.

I choose to speak the words of my heart, for fear they will be lost in the confines of my mind, thus clouding my vision

The ass can also be someone that is ignorant to the ways in which they act or respond to others criticism or advice. They may seem to agree on issues but do the exact opposite. Sometimes you may shake your head and wonder whether you have in fact lost your own mind, but you must consider your aurora when these personalities are not around.

There is often a moment of peace and serenity. Like the calm before the storm. You may sit on pens and needles upon their arrival, waiting for the shit to hit the fan as they say, and look for ways to excuse yourself early.

Another definition of the asshole could be those that are just out right rude. Have no consideration for other's feelings. They can't hold a conversation without interjecting inappropriate language or ghetto jargon.

Their approach to understanding is often anger, and fear. There is no admission

I choose to speak the words of my heart, for fear they will be lost in the confines of my mind, thus clouding my vision

of guilt, and an apology would be as if pulling teeth. These individuals feel the need to experience every scar, bruise, or consequence to bad decision making verses, learning from other's mistakes as well as their own.

Folk of the normal breed are shocked and mystified about the scrambled brains of the asshole and wonder what happened during their gestational period. As I have often quoted on face book, persons should really consider sobriety during their gestational period.

These individuals multiply as they join with others, thus creating another being. We may suggest finding partners for these persons so that they will help others in life deal with the short comings of these individuals, but with the attitude of the asshole they, of course, feel as if they are right and everyone else has lost their minds.

Now the complete moron, a new breed of assholes, has the Gaul to argue their

I choose to speak the words of my heart, for fear they will be lost in the confines of my mind, thus clouding my vision

ignorance and down play your intelligence by suggesting that you yourself are not up to par with today's growing changes. You may even be considered a hater because you do not agree with their destructive ways. When in question of the validity of their own argument they quickly shy away, suggesting that you wouldn't understand anyway, (basically noting and drawing to your attention that they don't know themselves), and parts company with you.

The ass resurfaces soon after, because friends of friends now having come in close contact with this being, have come to you in a fury telling all that they have said about you behind your back, and unleashing the drama he and or she has caused in their lives as well.

While you see some will reject the notion of the asshole we have all come in contact with one or two, in our day. The problem becomes an issue when these beings can't seem to get the memo that you

I choose to speak the words of my heart, for fear they will be lost in the confines of my mind, thus clouding my vision

THE REBIRTH OF MY SOUL,
2ND EDITION

just can't be bothered with the drama the asshole wallows in.

Some of us may have issues with understanding how to get away from these beings. We try so hard to help others when in need, however with my experience the asshole is pretty much just that a *Jerk*.

105 | *I choose to speak the words of my heart, for fear they will be lost in the confines of my mind, thus clouding my vision*

FORGIVE AND WISE UP

Forgiveness for life's torment may take you a lifetime to get over. However, you must be willing to forgive others in order to be forgiven for your own shortcomings. I am not really a superstitious person.

But, the statement, "What goes around comes around," does prove correct in many situations, to forgive and wise up shows growth in maturity.

Keeping in mind, that those you forgive should not mistake your kindness for weakness but; as a chance to regain trust, honor, and respect.

If you fall victim to continued mistreatment and deceptive behavior, then shame on them.

I choose to speak the words of my heart, for fear they will be lost in the confines of my mind, thus clouding my vision

"I DON'T HAVE TIME"

I recently ran into one of my old colleagues in the grocery store and I asked her what she had been up to.

She said, "Nothing much girl. Just work and home."

Sounds like a lot to me. That's pretty much what I am up to, besides school and writing which is my preventative medication. Well, Ms. Thing was quick to comment when I told her that I like to spend my spare time writing.

She was like. "Writing? Wow! I don't have time for that. What a life. I wish I could just sit around and journal."

I laughed and chose to choose my words carefully. I could have easily retorted with smart banter; but I said this. "I think

I choose to speak the words of my heart, for fear they will be lost in the confines of my mind, thus clouding my vision

we all are pressed for time. There are only 24 hours in the day. With my two boys running around, and the house work, homework, and my job it can be a hassle. But, I often take, if only 15 minutes, to write and reflect on my day. Perhaps create an agenda for the next day and cross some things off my list."

What is this I don't have time stuff anyhow. It isn't that you don't have time. Who does? It's what you choose to do with your time that separates productivity with laziness and procrastination. Which I know I am guilty of. After all we are only human.

"So what do you do in your spare time?"

"What spare time?"

She quickly sited that her work at home was never done and caring for the children and husband were often so over bearing, that she had to skip out for a drink at least twice a month. She went on to tell

I choose to speak the words of my heart, for fear they will be lost in the confines of my mind, thus clouding my vision

AIJA M. BUTLER

me that she loved her nights out on the town. Just last eve, she didn't get in until 3 the next morn. Now does this sound like someone who has no time? Not really! She just chose a different extra-curricular activity to relieve her stress. I told her to take care and parted company, ignoring the fact that she'd asked for my contact information to keep in touch. There didn't seem to be anything in common that I could relate or share with her any further. She thought that her time was more precious than others from the beginning of our reconnection. More-over, she reacted negatively to my choice of stress relief as opposed to hers. Maybe she thought that I wouldn't want to go out and get a drink with the ladies. Let my hair down and get my groove back, little did she know I can party with the best of them.

Just a hint for those reading this passage. Just because you don't like someone else's hobby doesn't mean you should play it down. I'm not sure if that is

I choose to speak the words of my heart, for fear they will be lost in the confines of my mind, thus clouding my vision

what she was doing with her whole, "Wow, wish I had time," sarcasm. However, I don't have the time... (wink), to spend my spare time analyzing her thought process on the matter.

The real reason for this entry is the statement, "I don't have time." I wanted to make sure that everyone understands that there is no time for all the chores we have either enlisted or been elected to complete. It is, once again, how we choose to spend the hours of the day. I could easily be writing this passage at 1 in the afternoon, while my boys are down for a nap. Instead of the piles of laundry separated on my kitchen floor. Or perhaps I could be out with the girls having one of those tasty blue electric lemonades, instead of the 3 chapters of Pharmacology homework due in 4 days. Catch my drift.

Some nerve of that broad. I do thank her for those ignorant remarks. I am internally grateful for her contribution to my madness,

I choose to speak the words of my heart, for fear they will be lost in the confines of my mind, thus clouding my vision

written within these pages. I don't know what we should call this little life after moment. How about Life after High School? It's nothing like running into the homecoming queen who happens to be 350 pounds to date, with *Twinkie* cream on her cheek, and taco sauce on her shirt. Or the football star, with the beer belly and receding hair that starts at the back of his neck. They got married you know. Ha! That was funny. I don't know, maybe it's the outcast in me talking trash. Take that Mr. and Mrs. *McDonald*.

I choose to speak the words of my heart, for fear they will be lost in the confines of my mind, thus clouding my vision

FANTASY LAND...

I laugh at myself and this entry because I know there are many people that believe that dreams and reality are worlds apart.

Well, I can tell you first hand, my dreams are becoming my reality. I too thought that fantasy=dreams.

We sell ourselves short by capping a ceiling on our "success". Its ok to dream and fantasize about ambitions or wants; but if we plan realistically, some of these fantasy's we dream of can actually come true.

This very book has been a fantasy and dream of mine for years. I have written many poems, and short stories, a novel even, but none of which I desired to see in print as much as I sought to see this project.

I choose to speak the words of my heart, for fear they will be lost in the confines of my mind, thus clouding my vision

LOL! My finance's, (fiancé) as we like to call one another jokes about this very dream of mine daily, "It's about time he says."

I admit it took a long time for me to believe in me. You can't begin to succeed until you begin to believe in your own ability's.

So I decided there were three fantasy dreams I would like to achieve in my 3rd decade of life. Hubby likes to call it my mid-life crisis, But here they are:

1.   Become an Author of a published Title,   whether it be poetry,   novel, short story collection, or inspirational motivation.

2.   Become a Model. Yes short, little ole me. I will take the time to get dolled up and have some modeling pictures of myself, professional taken.

3.   Singer, Songstress, I will produce, record, and sing a song that I have written myself.

I choose to speak the words of my heart, for fear they will be lost in the confines of my mind, thus clouding my vision

I encourage and challenge each of you to develop the goals and dreams that lay dormant in your fantasy lands.

Sometimes our reality shows get boring, in our daily professions. Just like our relationships with others we have to spice them up.

Spice up your lives with achievements big and small. Those joys and adventurous funnies, you can later share with your children.

I choose to speak the words of my heart, for fear they will be lost in the confines of my mind, thus clouding my vision

GOLDMINE...

You ever feel like you are the goldmine to someone else's dreams? You have the winning ticket that everyone else seems to be betting on. The ball is constantly in your court. To make a mistake would ruin the lives you hold dear to your heart. Sooner or later you will need to inform others that they must carry their own bags. You can't spend your life holding the luggage of others, when in fact you too are looking to have your own carried.

By which I mean... If your title in life isn't bell hop/boy, instruct them to get and tip their own.

Some folk are riding your coat tails and the tips are so non-existent. They can't even offer a word of advice to supplement monetary appreciation. Be the Goldmine to your own damn dreams.

I choose to speak the words of my heart, for fear they will be lost in the confines of my mind, thus clouding my vision

That way if things don't pan out, it's on you
and you own it...

*I choose to speak the words of my heart,
for fear they will be lost in the confines
of my mind, thus clouding my vision*

AIJA M. BUTLER

HONORABLE DISCHARGE

GOING THROUGH THE EMOTIONS

"Are you ready to leave?"

"Yes and No! I must admit I have become quite fond of the nursing staff. I'm afraid. I am so dependent on everyone, else to take care of my needs. I don't know how I am going to survive in the real world. Let alone take care of my daughter."

"Honey look out that window." Nurse Joyce demanded. "Do you see those blue skies and the wind blowing in the trees? Its Spring. A lovely time to enjoy Gods creations."

Nurse Joyce was always preaching. I was too, so it was like we had church every other weekend, when she was on duty.

I choose to speak the words of my heart, for fear they will be lost in the confines of my mind, thus clouding my vision

AIJA M. BUTLER

"You're right! I guess I can't help but worry. I have this fear of failure that I can't seem to shudder. What if I don't make it? The Doctor says I may not ever be the same. I have to be on medication for the rest of my life. I have so many disabilities. My goals and dreams may never take flight."

"Is this you talking, Aija. I am really confused. As much inspiration and motivation you have spread in these halls, is now a mystery to me. I don't understand. This doesn't sound like the Aija, I know and have grown to love. I hear those demons, that creep under our beds and tries to shake us. They shake and chase our feelings of confidence and comfort away. You can't let this change you. This too shall pass. You are a miracle. No Doctor or Nurse, for that matter thought that you would survive this disease. You are here for a reason. Make it count!

I choose to speak the words of my heart, for fear they will be lost in the confines of my mind, thus clouding my vision

IF IT CAN'T BE HELPED

You can't help those that do not wish to be helped. Your energy's will be better utilized if you relay the message to your higher power.

Lay your burdens down. Accept those things that you cannot change, and focus on the things you can.

Fixing the issues that can be corrected, often times opens doors to change those things that were previously damaged or shut.

I choose to speak the words of my heart, for fear they will be lost in the confines of my mind, thus clouding my vision

2003-AT DEATH'S DOOR

MILK SHAKE AND FRIES...

As I was saying at some point before, I don't remember much. My memories are awakened by similar events. Life experience tickles my brain. I know where my call button is and I am sure to remind my nurse about my pain meds; a half hour before they are to be administered.

The food is great. Vanilla milk shakes, for breakfast, lunch, and dinner. I am served on time and in bed. What a treat. I can't wait to add some hot fries to the menu. "Mcdonald's," French fries and a vanilla shake my all-time favorite treat.

I choose to speak the words of my heart, for fear they will be lost in the confines of my mind, thus clouding my vision

AIJA M. BUTLER

There was this nurse's assistant that made a huge boo-boo. According to my records anyway…

She brought me a tray of food by accident. I don't think I'd caught site of solid foods for at least a month. I was excited and scared at the same time. This was far too good to be true.

Sadly, it was the nursing assistant who not only got the name wrong she had the wrong room entirely. Talk about a real kill joy!

"Are you new?" I said between clenched teeth. I could have ripped the skin from her body, and beat her to the bone. You can only imagine, the amount of fire burning through my veins. My eyelashes were enflamed.

As my hunger pains played a soft harmonious violin.

I choose to speak the words of my heart, for fear they will be lost in the confines of my mind, thus clouding my vision

MRS. DOUBT-FIRE

All these wonderful ideas and accomplishments… You make effort after every effort to ensure the completion of your goals, and wham. You throw yourself a curve ball. What's the matter? Well you are elated about your accomplishments. Can't help but to smile at times… Even get teary eyed when you talk about your struggle; but you doubt your quality of your work.

I go through this, I think, every other day. I am a work that is always in evaluation status. My progress reports are reviewed monthly. I am still puzzled as to why I find fault in my own accomplishments. I fear the success about as much as I fear failure.

Mrs. Doubt-fire is a nick-name I call myself when I get into these moods. It has absolutely nothing to do with the concept of the movie. It just happened to fit my persona. I don't want to live up to Mrs.

I choose to speak the words of my heart, for fear they will be lost in the confines of my mind, thus clouding my vision

Doubt-fire. I'd rather be called "Dream Catcher".

I am in the continued pursuit of my dreams and I am catching hold of them every day. Relinquishing the doubt I occasionally have about my imperfections.

I choose to speak the words of my heart, for fear they will be lost in the confines of my mind, thus clouding my vision

ABANDONED SHIP

She has a need for attention. She was often seen show boating and complimenting herself for her good deeds.

"No one is perfect." This was her favorite line to quiet the crowd of spectators; trashing her name. It was another adventurous failed project; full of promise the new project of the day.

Remarkable social and youth servicing plan of action, budget, and of good use to the community; only her mind spun in circles. Her ideas would begin triumphantly and fail to come to pass.

The Paperwork complete, contracts, drawn, donations, public announcements, and marketing tools in place; even had the Federal tax identification number applied for and secured with nothing left but to put

I choose to speak the words of my heart, for fear they will be lost in the confines of my mind, thus clouding my vision

action behind words. Still, the ship settled in the calm of the sea.

One snag, a wrinkle, turns into frustration and ends in boxes, chronologically filed and pushed into a closet of well-organized ventures.

The point of this small insert showcases the importance of starting and finishing goals and aspirations. Task completion improves credibility and reliability.

I choose to speak the words of my heart, for fear they will be lost in the confines of my mind, thus clouding my vision

ARTS AND CREATIVITY

Children are creative artistic souls that need guidance.

Creativity can make you a star. It can also be a deal breaker if not properly cultivated, Dream big…but realistic.

I choose to speak the words of my heart, for fear they will be lost in the confines of my mind, thus clouding my vision

YOUR LEVEL OF UNDERSTANDING

Is initiative going beyond the call of duty? Has it anything to do with, doing things that you were not told to do? Or is it simply about handling one's own business without having to be told to do so?

I choose to speak the words of my heart, for fear they will be lost in the confines of my mind, thus clouding my vision

ALONG FOR THE RIDE

Life is a constant rollercoaster. So we must be up for its many challenging adventures.

When times get hard we must buckle our seat belts and meet our obstacles head first. In my times of trouble my thoughts were to break down and just give up, however I soon found out that if I could not fight for my own life, how could I fight for the lives of my children or better yet join with another?

You cannot claim to be an "us" if you have yet to become and I. Meaning. Individually we must know who we are and where we are going, before attempting to share our lives with others.

For quite some time I was unsure of where my life would end because of the

I choose to speak the words of my heart, for fear they will be lost in the confines of my mind, thus clouding my vision

illness I had been plagued with. With the constant haunt of its return, I hid under the confines of my bedroom with a pen and pad.

Journaling became my vise. I cursed my very being. Unable to grasp the thought that my life could truly end at such an early age, I pondered an escape. I questioned God.

Later, after months of uncertainty, I came to the conclusion that death would be easy; but I'd like to stay.

I had goals to accomplish, and though the pain was at times far too much to bear. I could endure it for a night.

My journals turned into my muse. I fell in love with written expression.

It challenges the mind to venture deep and pull out the true sensations of the heart. I could fight the battle and still loose, but at least I stood my ground.

I choose to speak the words of my heart, for fear they will be lost in the confines of my mind, thus clouding my vision

5 years now the disease is in dormant. It peeks every now and then and fear swells my lungs and stings my eyes.

There is a well of tears, but after a good cry I gather my tools of war and take my place.

How can you win if you don't bother to fight? We take bigger risks with our life, daily and unnecessarily, but give up when the time comes to go to battle.

Remember your cause. Delegate your tools of battle. Develop tough skin. And Go Hard for what you believe in.

I choose to speak the words of my heart, for fear they will be lost in the confines of my mind, thus clouding my vision

SWAG

Confidence: The feeling or belief that one can rely on someone or something; firm trust: "we had every confidence in our love, in one another", The state of feeling certain about the truth of something. "He is the truth, He is ready for love"

Faith: Complete trust or confidence in someone or something. If I am confident in him I am faithful

The cycle has restarted and I am faced with the two issues that seem to plague my journey with recovery. The words sickly are etched into my cerebral cortex and it singes the nerves in my feet and hands. They burn when I try to step towards positive venue. My fingers grow weary and cramp up when I raise my hands towards the sky or reach for a pen. My goals become tarnished, old and worn pieces of brass. The smell of defeat hovers around me.

I choose to speak the words of my heart, for fear they will be lost in the confines of my mind, thus clouding my vision

I am cooled by my contempt and rather confident in my ability to drop the ball. "Oh ye of little faith," This man of God told me.

This love that was greater than any love a human could possibly possess, so I often checked his pulse and bit into his flesh to see if his blood was as red as mine. I imagined in light his skin would take the look of diamonds sparkling under the sun's light. This love I often dreamed of…unconditional and one that resembled that of God. You see the love that God has for his children has no boundaries. Much like the mental connection I found in this physical being of human perfection. Not perfect as in fault…perfect in that with those faults bring forth, the appreciation of those pleasurable characteristics that are surely never to be taken granted of. This Rebirth moment is brought to you by a blossoming rose. It's blossoming, taking its full color and form, its thorns sharp and blood thirsty, confident. Now, reborn this rose is showered with all that it is needed to survive, the water

I choose to speak the words of my heart, for fear they will be lost in the confines of my mind, thus clouding my vision

and sun, and the faith that the well will never run dry.

I choose to speak the words of my heart, for fear they will be lost in the confines of my mind, thus clouding my vision

PARENTAL ADVISORY

I often sit and wonder what my parents felt as doctors told them my chances of survival were slim to none…

I couldn't imagine what it must have felt like to be told as a parent that nothing short of a miracle could save your child. All that is medically possible, gave no resolution. "You should think about making preparations," doctors advised. How do you make preparations to let loved ones go? Especially, your child. My stomach hurts now, just thinking of possible harm coming to my children. I often imagine my children as older adolescents and adults. I fantasize about how handsome and beautiful they have grown to be, and their "success".

It's hard to think about the what ifs. We could never be prepared. Being a parent is the most wonderful and heartbreaking experience you could ever endure. You are

I choose to speak the words of my heart, for fear they will be lost in the confines of my mind, thus clouding my vision

responsible for other's lives, and we as parents don't always have the answers. Sadly, we can't save them from the harsh realty's of this world. We love hard and sometimes they can be the meanest persons you have ever encountered. The only thing I can safely tell my fellow parents is this. "Put on the full armor of God. Pray over your children, and put them before the Lord. Cover them with His grace and mercy."

I choose to speak the words of my heart, for fear they will be lost in the confines of my mind, thus clouding my vision

SCARY MOVIE

Sometimes with my life's many, tormenting facets, I feel like I am a character in a scary movie. I get anxiety. My stomach bubbles, as if I ate a prepackaged sandwich off the roach coach in a desperate binge to cure hunger. I get so anxious when I hear news. Or figure out the outcome of a situation. Much like a scene from a scary movie. My chest aches. Almost as if someone is sitting on top of it trying to smoother me.

Just anticipating what will happen next, is worse when you already know the outcome. That in itself, can drive a sane person crazy. How do you attack the unknown, when you don't know when the unknown will strike?

It's all a mystery just like our lives. I hate the feeling of being in a scary movie. The suspense of it all, seems to raise my blood pressure and anxiety makes me uneasy. I love movies of adventure, and

I choose to speak the words of my heart, for fear they will be lost in the confines of my mind, thus clouding my vision

AIJA M. BUTLER

romance. There are always twists and turns. I am not knocking you scary movie lovers out there. Maybe you are the adventurous spontaneous type. Remember spontaneous, not stupid.

Take a moment to think about this passage. Decide what type of movie you are. Are you a risk taker? Is Adventure in your daily agenda, or are you too, a character in a scary movie, running away from the inevitable?

I choose to speak the words of my heart, for fear they will be lost in the confines of my mind, thus clouding my vision

THE SUPER INFECTION

You are suffering from a super infection. The infection of the mind you were previously diagnosed with has caused complications of the systematic operations in your mind causing another infection to develop.

Since, you have neglected the issues of ongoing problems in your life. The infection has not only multiplied into other facets of your life but, it has hyper developed. (modified itself), thus causing complete system melt down.

Get a hold of yourself. Tend to those nagging issues. You must be careful not to continue neglecting the issues. For they *will* get greater and multiply. The mind will be swarmed with an infectious disease. Which will become extremely difficult to treat. Just as those that manipulate drugs or do not adhere to their regimen, I have to be creative

I choose to speak the words of my heart, for fear they will be lost in the confines of my mind, thus clouding my vision

AIJA M. BUTLER

in relaying these messages to my readers. I want every one of different environments and cultures to understand the words written in and between these lines.

I choose to speak the words of my heart, for fear they will be lost in the confines of my mind, thus clouding my vision

FEELING TALL

Today my feet swirled out of bed and they planted themselves firmly on the ground. I stood tall and affirmed in my convictions. I wasn't restless in mind, wondering what the outcomes of this majestic decision making process would be.

I said "to hell with it all" and took a step towards trusting my ability's to succeed. Sure there were naysayers waving their flags of hate my way and cursing my moves towards greatness, but I say "onward" we will march towards victory. I was speaking to my hands and feet, of course, you now we are the only ones on the team. So if you will stand tall, because no one, and I mean no one, can have more faith in your ability's but you...once you find that strength to stand on your own, nothing will stand in your way.

I choose to speak the words of my heart, for fear they will be lost in the confines of my mind, thus clouding my vision

IF YOU LIKE IT I LOVE IT

I woke up today with a huge question hovering over me like a dark cloud of thunderous rain. That was deep I know; but seriously hear my inquiry.

What does the statement, "If you like it I love it…," truly mean? I say it often with regards to my siblings. As my brow creases during this entry I am forced to look into this matter. Aren't we saying that statement to basically say that we don't care? Or are we merely accepting the act, idea, or person, for who or what they are? I think the situation should be looked at on a case by case basis.

My case for instance, with the whole I don't like conflict business… is basically about my saying, "I don't want to be involved."

I choose to speak the words of my heart, for fear they will be lost in the confines of my mind, thus clouding my vision

Not that I don't care, or have an opinion, just that I don't wish to be bothered. It's a cop out. I don't want to unleash feelings and have to hash them out. Horrible I know, but I am so much better. I just had to admit that at times I could simply go along with the scheme of things just to avoid the talk, if you know what I mean.

It's not a good look, so in this journey to recovery, I am launching my very own campaign, yelling and screaming, "It's my party and I can cry if I want to."

If you ask me, I will tell you just how I feel," and I won't be blaming these sudden outbursts on turrets any longer either. I own my thoughts and opinions and I am happy to give it. Rest assured I won't be butting into business that isn't my own, unless I find that the activities those engage in is a direct threat to my wellbeing and danger to their health. Even then, it may be a toss-up. But those who ask my opinion must be prepared for what I dish out.

I choose to speak the words of my heart, for fear they will be lost in the confines of my mind, thus clouding my vision

METFORMIN MORNING COUNSEL...

"Who the hell am I anyway?"

Can you describe to someone who you are in one sentence? Your name doesn't count because that really doesn't matter, but who you are as a person, character, attributes rather.

I was sitting on the toilet thinking about this one morning. Don't even think about laughing. The toilet is my most sacred place. It's where all of my self-counsel takes place. I can rely on my conscience to take hold of my ID and superego and we have at it.

I choose to speak the words of my heart, for fear they will be lost in the confines of my mind, thus clouding my vision

Well, I owe all my counseling session to Metformin. As I am seated there, in between prayer hoping to gain some relief from the porcelain God, I can think about what I am going to do that day (Disney's, Phineas and Ferb), or simply ponder about life period.

My times in the bathroom alone are limited so, I must make use of my time. Sometimes I use these few moments to let off some steam, or have a good cry.

Well, any who, now that you know the background of my time with Dr. Phil, I asked the question about your ability to describe yourself to others, because I was puzzled with this same question. Hell I didn't know where to begin. A job application online asked me to describe myself in one sentence, and give my opinion as to why I was a good fit for the job. Ok….(drawing a blank). I didn't know how to answer the question. I literally didn't know where to start. Do I start listing physical characteristics as if I'm signing up

I choose to speak the words of my heart, for fear they will be lost in the confines of my mind, thus clouding my vision

for Facebook or Myspace? 31 year old African American Woman, with three kids. Sounds like I am looking for a date.

Am I to describe my abilities, educational background, current job title etc,. I was so puzzled I hit save for later and logged out. So during my time in the bathroom I began to practice. I asked myself the question. Can you, Aija, describe who you are in one sentence? It was quiet as a mouse in both my mind and the echo of the bathroom. I don't know if the question intimidated me. Or if that fact that I am long winded, and they asked me to describe myself in one sentence that threw me off.

Maybe I could drag the sentence along for about 100 words and put a period at the end? Ha! Ok so that was me stalling because I still can't answer this question. Which, we will have to answer by the end of this book. Be thinking about this question because it will come back to Haunt you. I would do the monster voice, but I don't know how to quite put that in words.

I choose to speak the words of my heart, for fear they will be lost in the confines of my mind, thus clouding my vision

THE DARKNESS

The night owl is my only friend

The time I throw caution to the wind

Odd thoughts and feelings I don't have to defend

The time I reflect and make amends

The dark hour is my time to shine

The time my pen marks this life of mine

My journal fills line upon line

Drowsing eyes, but to sleep there is no time

The midnight sky, the light of the moon

I cringe at the thought of sun rising too soon

I write in the night others come out in suns bloom

I choose to speak the words of my heart, for fear they will be lost in the confines of my mind, thus clouding my vision

AIJA M. BUTLER

Shucking and living there is no room

The stars in the sky are shining bright

As I am desperately writing my thoughts
before suns light

*I choose to speak the words of my heart,
for fear they will be lost in the confines
of my mind, thus clouding my vision*

THE REBIRTH OF MY SOUL,

I CAN'T LIVE FOR FEAR OF DYING

Afraid to live for fear of dying,

I draw a map of life,

I am unsure of where it will lead,

I have goals that I can see myself
accomplishing,

Though, I can't live for fear of dying,

 I am reminded that each day is not
promised,

I am afraid to live and take chances,

The risk of death is far too great,

Because I can't live for fear of dying,

I have this list…

A list of wishes, wants, and aspirations,

*I choose to speak the words of my heart,
for fear they will be lost in the confines
of my mind, thus clouding my vision*

I read them often,

But I can't live for fear of dying,

In a frustrated furry I crumble the pages of my journal,

I throw them in the trash,

The fear of death has threatened to take me,

I can't live for fear of dying,

After my loss of focus,

I gather my pen and pad and write them again,

I close my journal,

And I pray…

Dear Lord I am afraid to live for fear of dying what must I do, to lead these feelings astray?

I choose to speak the words of my heart, for fear they will be lost in the confines of my mind, thus clouding my vision

IT'S TRUE

IT'S TRUE

My Spirit is good

It just doesn't always win

My heart is sweet

The world just leaves a sour taste

My mind speaks of good cheer

I am just winded by negativity

Surrounding the banks of my habitation

My eyes smile

The tears blind my view

My cheeks blush excited for a new days
venue

Though the cold winds chaffing my face and
cutting my back change my consonance

It still remains true

*I choose to speak the words of my heart,
for fear they will be lost in the confines
of my mind, thus clouding my vision*

AIJA M. BUTLER

I am happy

Although I am worn

I am in good spirits

With each day I am reborn

*I choose to speak the words of my heart,
for fear they will be lost in the confines
of my mind, thus clouding my vision*

WHAT'S THE VERDICT...

I'm dying and this time a doctor told me so. I see life a lot differently now. I don't care for much arguing and if I disagree with the way others are acting and living their lives, I find it hard to comment. Could it be, at times that I don't care? Or is it possible that I feel that it may be best to live for the moment?

I feel like I am on trial. It's as if I witnessed a murder and I needed to come clean. I was the only witness. I was also the victim. I feel like I am locked in this dream, almost daily when the chest pain or migraines begin. I feel like the only way out is to surrender to the disease. My freedom is being ripped from under me. My dreams, that I finally started to complete were stolen. It's only a matter of time before I am crippled and bedridden.

I choose to speak the words of my heart, for fear they will be lost in the confines of my mind, thus clouding my vision

AIJA M. BUTLER

The worries happen and my cup falls to the floor and breaks. I am past the brink of self-destruction these days. I am angry with God, even these days. I am sitting now sweating bullets. My stomach is sure to explode. There begins the rocking. I could kill with the cut of my eyes. I am telling myself constantly to calm down. Everything will be okay. Then reality sets in and I realize that it's just the opposite. This is real. A real life tragedy.

The Verdict is in. The jury takes their seats. I stand to face my judge and jury and offer a plea of mercy. "If I could simply retain my sanity in light of your findings. I would like to throw my mercy unto the court. For with all that has taken place. I am lost. I am living a nightmare and I can't seem to get out. The nights and days run together. I am weak and without water. I am falling prey to the ways of this world."

Inching slowly, bending and swaying before passing out on the court's floor, I beg

I choose to speak the words of my heart, for fear they will be lost in the confines of my mind, thus clouding my vision

for a new cup and a fresh glass of water. For my soul is thirsty.

If I am to be whole again I must be replenished. No matter what I am faced with, there must be a light at the end of this tunnel.

Til the end…

Fill my cup so that I may quench this thirst, so that I can at least stand and fight, for as long as the fight is in me.

I choose to speak the words of my heart, for fear they will be lost in the confines of my mind, thus clouding my vision

BORN AGAIN THE RESURRECTION

COMING NOVEMBER 30, 2012

I choose to speak the words of my heart, for fear they will be lost in the confines of my mind, thus clouding my vision

INTRODUCTION

THE FINE PRINT

You ever suffer from an illness or discomfort of some sort and this remarkable commercial comes on that says, "Tired of feeling depressed, tired of just sitting around your home working the same dead-end job?" Or how about, "The cure is here. No more aches and pains…" You get up from your slump and scoot to the edge of your seat with all the excitement you can muster, and as you exhale you hear a man mumbling

I choose to speak the words of my heart, for fear they will be lost in the confines of my mind, thus clouding my vision

AIJA M. BUTLER

gibberish incoherently about the side-effects

to the drugs or activity.

The sulking continues, who wants to

risk the possibility of death due to side

effects of the drug, rather than the

symptoms? Life is much the same. When we

are born we grow.

Then we come of age, and our

rebellious natures choose paths both good

and bad. However as we humans plan for

our goals to become a reality, rarely do we

consider the fine print. The fine-prints I

speak of are the many snags, trials, and

tribulations that come along with this life

*I choose to speak the words of my heart,
for fear they will be lost in the confines
of my mind, thus clouding my vision*

journey. We want to be successful, we want to feel loved, and we naturally, well into our adult lives, would like the approval of both our peers and parents.

Sadly, life happens, things don't always come in order, and the fine-print on labels are often overlooked. So what's the stitch? What do we do with the life after moments that leave our mouths wide open with shock and dismay? Do we perhaps just throw in the towel and say better luck next time? Or do we stand and take our lives back, noting the mishap, and beginning anew. I don't down the fine-print. I embrace

I choose to speak the words of my heart, for fear they will be lost in the confines of my mind, thus clouding my vision

it. It causes me to pay attention to my goals, my dreams, my peers, and even my family.

The fine-print is a simple cautionary warning. Think of it as a wet floor sign right before you enter into a public restroom. You wouldn't just scurry in full speed, unless you happened to disregard the sign. Take a pilot for instance, there is a long list of to-do's before you are cleared to take off. You read, you study, you train, and then you soar.

This is what my life after honesty means. It is about all those leaps of faith we take, and those experience we encounter along the way. We are not always informed

I choose to speak the words of my heart, for fear they will be lost in the confines of my mind, thus clouding my vision

of the possible set-backs we may or may not

endure. But this is the sole purpose of this

memoir I share my quirky short stories

about my illness, my recovery, loss of

sensibility and my fight to achieve what

many said I couldn't. After all, 10 years ago,

doctors called my time of death 11/22/02 at

2:30am. What can I say, there was a change

in plans, God's plan. I am living proof.

There is a life after.

"Clear! We have a pulse…"

I choose to speak the words of my heart, for fear they will be lost in the confines of my mind, thus clouding my vision